THE PAIGE
GROUP

Dr. BJ Paige

"Your Network Is Your Net Worth"

Finding Your N.E.M.O.

NEW EMPLOYMENT MAKE OVER

THE 10 STEP WORKFORCE DEVELOPMENT GUIDE TO FINDING YOUR CAREER

BY

Dr. BJ Paige

Written by Dr. BJ Paige

Edited by The Paige Group

Cover Design by AW Graphics

Interior Format by Dupree Jonathan

Copyright © 2023 by Dr. BJ Paige

All right reserved content of this book should not be reproduced in any way or by any means without the consent of the Author in writing, except for brief excerpts or for critical reviews and articles.

> "He who says he can,
> and he who says he cannot,
> are both correct"
> -Confucius

TABLE OF CONTENTS

DEDICATION 9

FOREWORD 11

TESTIMONIAL 14

INTRODUCTION 16

WHO IS BJ PAIGE? 21

THE BACK STORY 24

THE PIVOT 34

TODAY 38

FINDING YOUR N.E.M.O 42

STEP ONE ....

WHO ARE YOU? 45

STEP TWO ....

WHAT DO YOU WANT TO DO? 70

STEP THREE ....

WHAT ARE YOU GREAT AT? 83

STEP FOUR ....

CAN YOU SUSTAIN THIS AS A CAREER? . 93

STEP FIVE..

WHO ELSE IS IN THIS SPACE?................ 101

STEP SIX..

HOW TO ENGAGE YOURSELF IN THE SPACE?.. 108

STEP SEVEN ....

BUILD YOUR LANE 114

STEP EIGHT ....

KNOW WHAT YOU KNOW 126

STEP NINE..

NETWORK... 131

STEP TEN..

GO GET YOUR CAREER............................ 138

THANK YOU 145

SHOUT OUTS 147

WHAT'S NEXT? ....

'HOW NOT TO GET FIRED?' 149

MY JOBS 151

MY BIO 154

DEDICATION

This book is dedicated to that person who is afraid of who they can be in their career!

I want to be intentional with dedicating this book to myself. Too often we take the back burner to everyone else – our responsibilities, our thoughts, our co-workers, and sometimes our superiors in the workforce.

I want to dedicate this book to you! To you, for investing in yourself. A great friend of mine has said to me over and over, that the most valuable asset we have is time and the most invaluable asset is influence. You took your time to purchase this book, read this book and take notes from this book, that does not go unnoticed. I hope that my influence offers you the confidence to share this with someone else who can use it.

FOREWORD

In any industry, or environment, where there are constant changes, I commonly give people this advice, "You need to know, what you don't know, when you don't know you need to know it." To do this though, you have to have a starting point of knowledge, and that starting point is knowing who and where you are at that moment. We know that who you are today, and who you were yesterday, doesn't define who you will be tomorrow, but having a starting point is a must.

BJ Paige's LIFE has helped him personally refine the processes of finding who you are, and while he has refined that, he also been the definition that your past doesn't define your presence. While he refined and defined both of those, through his journey in life, he found his NorthStar! That NorthStar was BJ finding and identifying who BJ was personally, then molding who BJ was personally into a purpose that became a profession. By combining who he was as a person, with a professional purpose, BJ developed his foundation and found his "WHY"! We've all been blessed that BJ's WHY, and who he is at his foundation, is his unique ability to utilize his journey in helping others lay their foundation, find their NorthStar, develop their WHY, and launch a career.

If you are finding YOU, and your WHY, or you are helping others find themselves or their

WHY, you found the right book and you definitely found the right author. Finding Your New Employment Make Over, your N.E.M.O, is going to change your life. Based on BJ's truth and experiences, and his experience in reaching tens of thousands of people across the United States, he's put the process to finding your NorthStar to pen and paper.

Finding Your N.E.M.O provides the guidance and tools to begin charting a personal and professional course, it's what people need to find their NorthStar, and it's what people need to finding their WHY and their professional purpose. Start today and never stop!"

-Walter Simmons,
President & CEO of Employ Prince George's

TESTIMONIAL

"I have continued to watch BJ Paige climb the ladder in workforce development since his initial days of gathering young leaders that were searching for community outlets. When asking him to lead our Flikshop School of Business classroom, he led workshops successfully while coaching our participants to success. BJ's superpower is building leaders and introducing them to the workforce with an innovative approach."

-Marcus Bullock, CEO,

Flikshop

"There are so many reasons that I'm excited to share how much BJ has influenced the culture of what workforce development is today. As an expert who works with so many people transitioning their professional careers, I have watched BJ be consistent in changing the lives of so many people in their career hunt. I would be happy to introduce anyone that I know to utilize the tools that he offers to so many other future leaders in the workforce"

-Richard Drosin, CEO,

RD Resumes and Career Coaching

INTRODUCTION

I know you love your job, and you make a million dollars a year, right? WRONG! Most of us find great jobs that does great things for the life we live, however most struggle to find what we all call a career. The key is to keep going until you find yourself what I refer to as your *'career for life'*!

As a top workforce development specialist, every day I help people build themselves to their career for life. But what is a career for life? A career for life is more than a job, heck, it's more than a career. A career for life is when your superpower matches the opportunity for you to do what you are good at, what comes natural to you and somehow you now get a chance to do that every day and get paid which will allow you to take care of you and your family while doing it, for the rest of your life. Your career for life is the career that is bursting at the seams of all things that represent you! The hardest thing to do is find it.

It's like finding N.E.M.O. When you find yourself stuck in the day to day, unfamiliar situations, having to fight out of that, and knowing you got yourself into it; you can't just comply, you must keep going. Then you have people trying to find you, to help you. You try to do everything you can, to realize it was only you that you had to prove it to. You have people who are looking to help you and can't find you because you're in all of the wrong places, focused on the wrong things.

In life it is so many things that stop us from doing our best and so many barriers along the way that block us at the wrong time. From early on, we have always been taught to be successful, like go to college to get a degree, then find a good job with good benefits, work 20 years, and retire. Or you can be successful by going into the military, serve your country, serve 20 years, and retire. Or how about find a trade program, get your certification, work 20 years, and retire. Or even, be your own boss and start your entrepreneurial journey of working for yourself. No, it's this one, just find you a good 9 to 5 and do your best at that job until something comes along.

They all sound so simple right? According to those rules, if you follow any one of those five plans, everything will be perfect, and you will be successful! But what is success? No really, take a minute and answer that, what is success? There is no legit answer that should be given from anyone but you. Success is what you want it to be. Success in your career is to control your career. This does not mean quit your job and make a life change today. To me it simply means that if I want to make my life better, I am in control. One thing that I learned growing up about control is, the one and only thing that you have control over is you. You control your thoughts; therefore, you now control your actions. You are in control of the next second, the nest minute, and the next hour; you are in control of what happens next!

You are probably asking yourself, who is this guy BJ Paige to tell you what to do? What makes him the expert in this space of workforce development? Glad you asked! You deserve to know who you are dealing with, let's dive in. This guide is the story of myself, Dr. BJ Paige, and how I tied my personal and professional experiences to provide you with the 10 steps to finding your career. Within these 10 steps, sometimes the hardest step is not steps one through ten, but the most important step of 0 to 1. Today you have completed that step, today you begin to Find Your N.E.M.O.

WHO IS BJ PAIGE?

I am Dr. BJ Paige, a top Workforce Development Motivational Speaker who focuses on changing the lives of youth and young adults. I was born in the Nation's Capital, Washington, DC, and I am a proud native of Prince George's County, Maryland. I am a proven trailblazer in the field of Workforce Development, where I help people find their career. My passion is to help underserved youth and the returning citizens population, where I am now the first ever Returning Citizens Liaison for Prince George's County, Maryland. I have tons of accolades to include specializing as a Master Facilitator,

Life Coach, National Association of Workforce Development Professionals (NAWDP) member and I am a Veteran of the United States Air Force where I spent my time in Security Forces. I have been recognized as one of the DMV (DC, Maryland, and Virginia) 48 Men of Power and also the Greater Washington Community Foundation Emerging Leader Award, the inaugural award of its kind.

I spent over 12 years serving the people in my community. Here are a few highlights, I was a 2018 candidate for Prince George's County Council, District 7; I was named Top Forty Under 40 for Prince George's County; I was honored with The Maryland General Assembly Official Citation Awardee for my Community Commitment; awarded the Citizen of the Year from Omega Psi Phi Fraternity – Gamma Pi Chapter; presented the Real Good People Award WPGC 95.5 and a ton of honors to speak to my work in the community. With my focus on career development in higher education, early in my career, I worked as the Executive Assistant to the Health Sciences Executive Team at Howard University under the guidance of President Wayne A. I. Frederick. I functioned as a Youth Career Consultant for Prince George's Economic Development Corporation and Youth Business Consultant for the KEYS (Knowledge Equals Youth Success) Program at Prince George's County Economic Development Corporation.

I have partnered with several civic based programs feeding the underserved, worked with YAP (Youth Advocate Programs); I was the NAACP Youth Council Advisor – Prince George's County Branch; worked as the Executive Director for Run Hope Work, a nonprofit for at-risk young adults ages 20-24 in Washington, DC's toughest areas in Ward 7 and Ward 8; Founder of Boys 2 Bowties, a mentor program with emphasis on helping young men grow from adolescence to adulthood; functioned as the DC Metro Director for the Baltimore-DC Metro Building Trades Council; and served as the Associate Director at Flikshop School of Business, where we helped prepare students for life as an entrepreneur in the gig economy.

I have had the proud experience of working in about 15 different industry sectors within over 30 different organizations.

Sounds like a full career, right? Well, let's hear about the back story.

The Back Story

The transferable skills started when I was 16 years old. Growing up with a single mother, in a small area called Forestville, Maryland, home of the best snickerdoodles in the world. It was me, my mother, and my younger sister, she is seven years younger than me. I was in my junior year in high school, and I was a sports superstar. I played football at my high school and AAU basketball, where I excelled in both! During this school year was my first year of organized high school football and I started receiving the college scouts, viewing my play on the field, that people dream of, and I was traveling the country winning in the AAU basketball circuit. I was Homecoming King and was just the all-around cool kid within the crowd.

On a Friday night, I went out on a double date with a group of friends. We went to the movies and later we met up at the golden arches, McDonald's. While there, I specifically remember ordering a #1 with no pickles. Before we received the food, I turned around and we were now I was in the middle of a big group fight. After the fight someone got shot, and I am thankful to God that he did not die.

When I got home, I stayed in the house for two days until Monday morning for school. Monday came and I was not ready for what was about to happen next.

I went to school and was greeted by my Administrator and three police officers were at the door. Next thing I know, I was in a grown man's jail at 16 years old. I slept for three days straight until I was released. Knowing my innocence, I was thankful to be back home after witnesses confirmed my innocence to the crime. I rushed back to school, only to find out that I was expelled from Prince Georges County Public Schools. WHAT!?!? Expelled meant not being able to attend school in any Prince George's County, which also meant no football scholarships, and no NFL career, in my young mind. My mother did an amazing job raising me, but she never dealt with anyone being kicked out of school, so she didn't know what to do. She quickly enrolled me in DC Public Schools, and I was expelled again on the first day for fighting. As soon I walked in, this dude called me a "Maryland Bama". At that time in my life, where I'm from, that is one of the worst things you could have called someone not living in DC. Now, what to do? No high school options, so I was enrolled in home school. Home school didn't last long either; Don't Ask! However, I was super determined to graduate on time and honestly did not know how this would end up for me. We reached out to my father who at the time lived far away in Gaithersburg, Maryland. I went from being the oldest of one sibling to the oldest of seven siblings really quick. I remember doing everything I could possibly do to graduate on time. All I knew was that the sooner I graduated, the sooner that I could find a job and make it in this world as an adult.

Next, I had to do what I had to do and graduate on time, mission accomplished! Now that I graduated, I had to find a job. But how? With no mentor, no college, no trade, and no options, what was I to do? After talking with my mother, she agreed to sign over my rights at 17 years old and allow me to enter the United States Air Force. I had no life skills, no career goals, or no vision for my future. Joining the military was one of the best decisions that I have ever made. Stationed at Barksdale AFB, Louisiana, I learned so much and met so many wonderful people. Some of whom I am still close with to this day. However, by the time I was 20, trouble found me once again, and I was incarcerated in military confinement and soon kicked out of the military. When I felt helpless, I fought to get better. I don't know what I was thinking about back then, but what I did know was that I had to find a job, so no that was my career home! Looking back at it today, I had what one would say a Double PTSD (Post-Traumatic Stress Disorder). PTSD coming home from the military to the real world and PTSD coming home from jail with a record.

PTSD may occur in people who have experienced or witnessed a traumatic event or circumstances. One may experience this as physically or emotional harm or life-threatening, and may affect your mental, physical, social, or spiritual well-being. Some examples include car accidents, terrorist acts, combat, natural disasters, sexual assault, historical trauma, intimate partner violence and maybe even bullying,

In the past, PTSD has been known as "shell shock" during the years of World War I, but PTSD does not just happen in combat. PTSD can occur in all people, of any ethnicity, or culture. PTSD affects about 3.5 percent of U.S.

adults every year. The lifetime of PTSD in adolescents ages 13 -18 is 8%. It's estimated that 1 in 11 people will be diagnosed with PTSD in their lifetime. These three ethnic groups – Latinos, African Americans, and Native Americans are too often unreasonably affected and have higher rates of PTSD than any other ethnic group.

People with PTSD have intense, disturbing thoughts and feelings related to their experience that last long after the traumatic event has ended. They may relive the event through flashbacks or nightmares; they may feel sadness, fear, or anger; and they may feel detached or estranged from other people. People with PTSD may avoid situations or people that remind them of the traumatic event, and they may have strong negative reactions to something as ordinary as a loud noise or an accidental touch.

Researchers have even come to find that incarceration can lead to PTSD, meaning that even after serving a sentence, many people continue to suffer the mental effects. This is why I say, it is safe to say that I had to deal with the unfavorable diagnosis of Double PTSD. It was not an easy transition for me however I had to push through, I had to find my career; for my family and most importantly, for myself!

Immediately, I began to start my job search by applying for at least 20 jobs a day, consistently. I began to learn what different job descriptions looked like, what the job requirements were, how much they paid and how many positions for hire each company had. I would research the companies, their Human Resources Department, their Directors, their culture, their mission, and their vision; all so I would learn just what they were looking for. You can say that my full-time job, was finding a full-time job. I started walking into places asking to speak to the manager just in case someone called out of work that day. Later, I was hired to work the front desk at a hotel. This was an easy job to me, I would be nice to people, take their form of payment and make sure they had everything that they needed while they stayed at the hotel. I began to learn the Front Office Manager's job by asking to work with him on his shift. As soon as he thought about leaving, he openly welcomed me for that position. I still felt that I needed more money to support myself and my family. I applied for the night audit position, and this would allow me to find another part time job to work during the day while I worked at the hotel at night. It took me a while, but I was hired at the local gas company as a meter reader. The timing was perfect because I could go to work at the hotel at 10pm and get off at 6am. and get to work at the gas company by 7am. At the gas company, once you've done your route, you're done for the day. I would be done, no later than noon. I would be home by 1pm with just enough time in the day to get some rest. This went on for over a year and I still was not happy. I was dead tired, and the money wasn't adding up. I felt helpless so what did revert to? I fought to get better! I went back to applying for jobs daily.

I ended up working in every career field that you can think of. You already know about hospitality and utility, well add these to the list – I was a car salesman, grocery store manager, retail (3x's), apartment leasing, education, finance, nonprofit, economic development, and entrepreneurship. All of that in a ten-year span. I worked with just over 15 companies in ten years, but I met a lot of people and was sure to treat every person with the highest respect. You can't outwork relationships. You can't put a price on a conversation with someone. And you never know when the person holding the door for you could be the same person with the name on the reserved parking spot out front.

Remember success can be dropped in your lap at any given time; however, for most of us it's when preparation meets determination. There's no good or bad time to start; there is right now. What's on your mind today? Today could be the beginning for you and your new career

The Pivot

In sports, such as basketball and football, you learn a lot about teamwork, commitment, competition, and techniques. All these qualities are important, however the greats in the sport all have high level technique. I'd like to call this time with you, The Pivot. In basketball, pivoting is most common when a player avoids a defensive player and there is an opening to take a shot, make a pass, or dribble. You can't lift your pivot foot off the floor until you do one of the three and you can't change your pivot foot once it's established. In this time in my life, I was the ball handler and I had to make a pivot.

I was feeling better in my professional career but still not where I knew I wanted to be. I was the Founder and Executive Director of a local nonprofit called Boys 2 Bowties. We helped young men ages 8-18 transform from adolescence to adulthood. We were doing amazing work! We were everywhere, in the communities, the schools, on TV, social media, everywhere! We changed a lot of lives in our community and encountered over 700 plus youth in our tenure. We had an annual Back 2 School event called Project Peace. This was a free community event where we hosted a huge cookout with entertainment and a pool for all age groups and provided school clothes, school supplies, haircuts, and hair styles to the youth. Each year we provided over 1,000 free book bags filled supplies to the community at large. This was all done for the community by the community.

This initiative made so many headlines that I was asked to come to Prince George's County Economic Development Corporation for a partnership meeting with their President. By now, you can already imagine how excited we were to have the support of such a huge organization, especially compared to our grassroots community approach. While there I was asked about workforce development. I mean to be direct; this is what was said "you should get into workforce development; do you know what that is?". And let me be clear, I had no idea what it was then but surely, I said yes. I guess, the gentleman asking had a hunch that I had no clue, so he began to tell me. Though the term workforce development has different perspectives, in this space it is an element of economic development. It is a wide range of programs and policies that create a valuable workforce that can support current and future industries.

Workforce Development programs can help a person sustain economic security. In short workforce development initiatives educate and train a person to be prepared and ready to meet the needs of an industry and the businesses in the workforce to cultivate financial growth, otherwise, a career. By the time he finished talking and I provided my experience in helping the youth and young adult population over the years, I was offered a new job on the spot. I was now a Youth Career Consultant, under the umbrella of workforce development. Mama, I made it! I now get paid to do what I had been doing for free for years.

But here's the thing, after spending years to find my new career, I found it! Here's where the rubber meets the road, the position was a $28,000 pay cut from current job. What was I to do? This is what I been looking for. How will I take care of my family? More important, what would my wife think? Well, I'll a tell you what she said, "oh, you can't take that job…". I paused for a minute and just told her I would talk to her later. She called me back a few minutes later to say that I should chase my passion and we will work out the finances. To be honest, what I was feeling at this point was doubt. Was this enough income? Was this really my passion? Was this a career field that I could make an honest living? Well, we would soon find out.

TODAY

Looking back at that journey is a glimpse of the reality; the reality of focusing on your strengths, chasing your passion, and not stopping until you are successful in your own eyes. I am excited to share what I view success to be; I am highly successful; and still looking for more. Some people may say that I am good, and why would I want more. We are put on this earth to be plentiful and are due the favor of overflow if we put the work in, it is ours if you continue, and not to give up. Today I travel the country, and soon the world, speaking to people about the importance of focusing on your career for life. I also provide workshops for professional leaders at organizations in the space of workforce development, staying innovative and connecting to the underserved communities.

What is your career for life? A career for life is the full alignment. It's when your passion matches your life values. Your life values are what ultimately makes you happy and now, they make you money. It's like the saying, once you do what you love, you'll never work another day in your life again, but on steroids. That's where I am now. I am literally living in a dream. Each day of my life is revolved around the word "help", I help people from underserved communities find their strengths, find what makes them happy, and I help them turn that thing, into their career for life.

NOW IT'S TIME FOR YOU!

FINDING YOUR N.E.M.O.

Earlier I said you control your thoughts; you control your actions. Today you start controlling you! Today you start Finding Your N.E.M.O. - Your New Employment Make Over. We will begin the journey of 10 steps that will help you forever. That will help you find your career for life! Today we begin to find your career and you get to live out your dreams. We will talk through the 10 Steps to help you. These 10 Steps start now, with the most important unspoken step that you have already taken; that is step zero to one. Sometimes the hardest but most important step is starting, and you have already committed to that. I can make one promise – that is you will have to visit this book more than once. Everything else is up to you and how much sweat equity you put in these steps. Do not underestimate the amount of difficulty you are going to face in this process. Do not shy away from the amount of self-determination that you will have to put into the process. Now let's get started, grab your note pad, and let's get you on your way to Finding Your N.E.M.O!

The Ten Steps To Your N.E.M.O.

- Step One: Who Are You?
- Step Two: What Do You Want to Do?
- Step Three: What Are You Great At?
- Step Four: Can You Sustain This As A Career?
- Step Five: Who Else Is in This Space?
- Step Six: How to Engage Yourself In The Space?
- Step Seven: Build Your Lane
- Step Eight: Know What You Know
- Step Nine: Network
- Step Ten: Go Get Your Career

STEP ONE

WHO ARE YOU?

Not what is your name, but what are you made of? What are all of the pieces to your puzzle? How are you wired? How were you raised? And yes, these things matter to what you will do as we look for your career for life, trust me. To find your N.E.M.O. you have to first know who you are and who you are starts from when you went from a child to adolescents. Though that does change many times over while becoming a seasoned adult all the way through whatever your retirement may look like. Let's start with me, BJ Paige.

Who is BJ Paige? BJ Paige was smart, joyful little kid that was raised by a single mother, in a community where that seemed to be the common household capacity. My father was not really in my life, heck his father wasn't in his life either, but that's beside the point, we're talking about me, right? He was around some, but I didn't see him for months at a time, and sometimes years.

When we did speak, he would promise things and not follow through. Simple things like him saying he was going to call me back or pick me up; but he never would, he had me waiting for-ever. I was waiting for something that just never would happen without me initiating and continuing to try. Even then, I can count on both hands the number of times that it happened. Those days that I didn't see him hurt me whether I realized or not at that time. The holidays that I didn't get to see him left broken promises as far back as I can remember. Those times left me to have a cold heart, frequent separation from others, and commitment issues. Up to the age of 16, my mother raised me and my sister as good as she could. In my eyes, she did an outstanding job.

Growing up, I was always first to raise my hand in class, first to volunteer to do something, and always picked first when playing basketball and football. I was in the church choir, and I played in the church choir band, because I wanted to do anything not to sing. I always had the word of help in everything that I done. I wanted to help my classmate be better. I always wanted to help my friends around the neighborhood as well, whether it was to help them cut grass, helped make sure they ate if they had no food, and helped them get out of trouble. So that's what it looked like as a child for me.

Around the 6th grade, my mother did something for the neighborhood that was never done. It was something that we didn't really have, and something that we really wanted. It was the closest thing to what you would call the Boys and Girls Club for us. Mom bought one of them roll out basketball courts, you know, the one you put the water at the bottom and find a brick to put on top, so it won't fall. It was the best thing we had other than the playground, as a safe haven for the community. Then she let us use the garage and driveway as the rec room and weight room. Just like most kids that learn from their parents, my mother, is what led me to be where I am today.

My mom has a passion to help others; she just wanted to help all the kids in the community have a safe place to play basketball. Every day the whole neighborhood took turns to make sure water was in base of the basketball court and we were off to play ball right there in the middle of the street.

It's funny thinking about it now as an adult because we would hold up so much traffic and nobody went crazy about it. I guess because we were all in one place, doing our best to stay out of trouble. Adolescence really began there for me, I learned how to really play basketball there, we started a band there, learned how to play cards there, started my entrepreneur spirit was started; I sold snacks, Kool-Aid, popsicles, chicken nuggets, whatever kids in the neighborhood wanted to be happy. Every parent in the neighborhood knew where their child would be from the time, they got off the school bus to the time they got in the house. I saw myself helping the entire neighborhood, that's what it looked like in my early adolescence.

Because of the basketball court, I was kind of well-known by the time I reached middle school. I played for the middle school basketball team, and I received the Most Athletic award. During middle school I was kind of forming into the "cool guy". Every time something happened whether good or bad, you got it, that guy BJ was involved.

I would always want to see if I could influence to help better whatever that situation was. I wanted to help somebody get a lunch that didn't have lunch money, I wanted to help somebody get out of a fight if they were being picked on. I wanted to help somebody get an A in class by studying more or I wanted to help somebody find a ride home just to stay after school. I just wanted to help people any way that I could! Next, I was off to high school, and this is where some people grow up faster than others. There's a lot of people in one place, a lot of emotions, a lot of testosterones, a lot of growth and one of the toughest transitions most have.

I believe we all go through at least three transitions in life; youth to adolescence, adolescence to young adult, and young adult to adult. Some people have the privilege of more transitions in life than others, whether that be marriage, parenthood, or other transitions in your professional space. But this high school transition was special for me, it was a transition where so many of us young adults were able to go to school with way more people from different neighborhoods, than those in middle school. More people, more teachers, more eyes on each one of us. Nothing changed in my want to help, this time help was magnified. I might have changed my approach a little bit but continued to help people with homework, continued to help people that were less fortunate, but overall continued to just help people. That should not have been where I started helping people with fights, but it was.

By now, not only was I known for being smart, being athletic, being good in class, being cool with the teachers; I was also known for fighting. Everybody in the area high schools knew me from one neighborhood to the next neighborhood. This time in my life was a great lesson around help. The lesson was sometimes how you can only help people to a certain point, but you have to allow them to continue on their own journey sometimes. You can help from a-far without being so controlling or hands on. Sometimes you can give someone the tools, then you step away. The reason why I say that was a lesson because this is the time where my passion for helping others unfortunately caused me to be put in jail, expelled from school, and lost my scholarships at the age of 16.

As I reflect again on how everything transpired, I remember clearly that I went on a double date to the movies and McDonald's with a few friends. Being Mr. Popular, everyone knew who I was. I also remember someone saying something to our girlfriends and that was the start of a big group fight that led to someone getting shot. It was the four of us against who knows the amount of people. Looking back at it today maybe it was only four of them, but when we pulled up, all we heard was others say the police were coming and we left. By the end of the fight, I'm back home and my phone was ringing off the hook. I ignored the calls all weekend. By the time I got to school Monday, I thought that the situation was over, since it was not during school hours and not on school grounds. I'm walking towards the front door of the school and I'm eye to eye with a school Administrator and I see the police next to him. I'm a little nervous but I don't know what happened, but I know I was now under arrest. Because of that one fight that led to so many things in one night, I was expelled from Prince George's County Public Schools. That is the reason why my scholarship offers rescinded.

Until the police figured out what was going on with that case, of course the colleges did not want that type of representation at their schools. So, to try to save a high school career, my mom and I tried to go to another school district, District of Columbia Public Schools. Unfortunately, on my first day of registration a small confrontation occurred, and the Administration there said since I was already coming from a situation where this is what caused me to get expelled that I could not come to this jurisdiction at all. I know, I know, that was not smart. This fight was from myself being frustrated with losing my scholarship.

After being expelled from two school districts and wanting to desperately graduate on time, we looked into home schooling. Home schooling was cool except; I was not used to being with a stranger one on one with no accountability to do actual work. Soon I realized that home schooling was not ideal for me, so I was advised to reach out to another school district, Montgomery County Public Schools. Sometimes people guide you to open your eyes more to see that there are different things out there for you. I reached out to that school district and was accepted. I had to drive so far just to go to school, like over an hour with traffic. I had to find someone that lived out there. That person was my father. As I said earlier, I did not have a real relationship with him, but he wanted to help, and I needed the help. So off to my senior year of high school I went, to live with my father.

With my stubbornness, or strong mind; you can pick either one for the context of my message, I did not last long with my father. We bumped heads so many times, we argued, we cussed, and I left. I was fortunate enough to meet a great family in that short journey and moved with them to finish my senior year, on time. Sometimes we just don't know where our paths will take us or who will be there to help you; just be in position to accept the help from friends and strangers. This may be the next move, to take you to your best move. If I would not have moved with this family, who knows what would have happened next.

As the school year came around and I questioned with being the new guy, would my past follow me, the good and the bad? The good is that I played football and basketball, both starting point guard and cornerback. I noticed that I did not have to try hard to fit in. Eventually I became the cool guy at the new school, but unfortunately the same reputation followed me of being the bad boy. This school was a different space and different from the norm, my norm I should say. I love that it was primary rural culture, full of so much diversity. How I acted and reacted with issues in this school year was different. I saw that my reputation that followed me was not what made me. I noticed that I didn't have to try hard to fit in. Everything that I've done at that school in one year of my senior year of high school, was exactly what I always wanted to help my old neighborhood with.

I was out there in a whole different world with new people that I did not know, I showed them how to be better when it came to treating people that's not from where you are, people that look different from you, and to treat them just as good as you would treat anybody else in your family or community. It was easy to say that this year of high school was where I was out of my comfort zone of traditional urban life, to a more diverse population of life. That time taught me some valuable lessons on people and different cultures regardless of where you are from or how you were raised. We all have good people from all sides of the earth, even if they weren't raised the way I was raised.

I ended up graduating on time and I didn't really have a mentor or a real father figure outside of my biological father. I ended up not getting my scholarships in football and I didn't know about the options of junior college, redshirt freshman options, and even the option to just stay back a year to better my opportunities to regain my football scholarship because of my troubles. I ended up going to the United States Air Force and honestly it was one of the best decisions I ever made. I graduated high school at 17 because I have a late birthday in October, so yes, I ended up graduating high school entering the military at 17 years old. My mom had to sign a release of rights waiver for me to go to United States Air Force. This is where adulthood kicked down the door fast.

While in the Air Force I learned a lot. Up to this point and time in the Air Force, everything I've ever done good revolved around the word "help". Often, I will find myself doing what was right for others before doing what's right for me. I believe that all of that was already in me prior to the Air Force but the Air Force kind of pushed that to another level for me. While in the Air Force, I could not get a Top-Secret Clearance and I don't know if it was because of my troubled background or because the troubles in my family history. I was stationed at Barksdale Air Force Base, Louisiana where at the time was primarily a nuclear weapon base. I went in the Air Force as what they call open general, open general is when you enlist and you're not quite certain what career field you're going to be in, and the military finds the job which best suits the military. In my case they needed Security Forces, so I was a 17-year-old guy from the Washington, DC area, and straight to Louisiana. I don't know if this was good or bad for young BJ at the time. I had to grow up fast and growing up fast was some of the wonderful things that happened while in the Air Force.

I met a lot of great men and women along the way that led me to one of my best friends that

I still have to this day. He will never admit that when we met, I beat him up and we've been best friends ever since. There were a lot of major accomplishments for me within Security Forces at such a young age, carrying a weapon, protecting, and serving the people on such a large military institution and yet I still find myself in the space of help; and in the space of trouble all the same. In the Air Force there is certain things that you just cannot do! What caused me to get kicked out fell under Uniform Code of Military Justice (UCMJ), as an Article 134.

This article is like no other charge in the civilian world. As a matter of fact, a lot of people call it the "catch all" article in the military because they kind of throw anything in their article to defend the best interest of the United States Uniform Code of Military Justice. What I did in the military did not break any law in the civilian world, but I'll explain.

The year was 2001 and my son was in the womb. I really believe with me growing up without my father or a father figure, and not having a clear thought of what a strong father would be, I was scared! I found myself looking in the mirror at myself, looking at me in the military. My rank was an E-4 at the time, and I said to myself "this is not it, this not enough money for me to take care of my child". I remember feeling that I needed to do something, but I didn't do nothing too crazy. At least, I didn't think it was crazy at the time. Just like high school, I was the guy on the base that everybody knew. As a matter of fact, I was the face of the base when you came through the main gate. Long before how the military has it now, with the mixture of contractors and active-duty Security Forces, there was this thing at that base gates called Ambassador Gate Guards. That was me. We were a special crew of Security Forces who were dedicated to entry points of the base. And with Barksdale Air Force Base being such a high-profile base, we had all eyes on us. If you came through the gates of that base, nine times out of ten, it was me waving you on, saluting you, and all that good stuff. I was even on the front of the base magazine. So, guess what, because everybody knew me, and just like high school, the military looked to use that opportunity to set an example for other military members behind me. In short, I made the military look bad, I was the image of a military member in uniform while committing a crime.

In that, this is where my Article 134 was given to me, it was said that I brought discredit to the armed forces. When the military took me to court, I had the option to fight it or just let it be, me again being young and not having proper guidance or network, I went with the court decision and ended up being locked up and kicked out the military with a felony.

In my humble opinion, today, I don't think that was my smartest decision but I'm glad it happened when it happened. I took a plea deal which punished me in so many ways. I was reduced in my rank or what most know as my pay scale, locked up in military jail, 1/3 of my pay was taken while in jail, kicked out the military, and given a Bad Conduct Discharge (BCD). Did I think I had been given a harsh punishment? Yes, super harsh looking back at it. I don't think anyone deserves that much punishment as a 20-year-old young man who joined the military at 17 years old. I can still remember the smell of the jail. It was like a dirty wet mop mixed with an outhouse at summer camp, let's just say, it wasn't nice. I remember having to march and follow military orders as if I were in basic training all over again. I remember being handcuffed and it being mandatory to sidestep in the cafeteria line, just to eat my three meals a day. This was by far, the toughest time in my life.

Here's the kicker, the one thing that always got me into trouble each time in life was defending my sense of help for myself.

At the time I just felt defeated because of what happened, and I ended up being in confinement, military jail. During that time is where I had a lot of time to think, I had a lot of time to decide to think of what I wanted to do for my life and what I wanted to do next with my professional career when I got out of this trouble.

When I finished my jail sentence, I was out and ready to find myself. I was kind of already on to the next phase of separation. I came back home to Prince George's County, Maryland from Louisiana out of confinement and out of the military. At this point, I was definitely going through double PTSD.

In most cases, people that transition home from the military have some sort of PTSD and if you've been in military, you have been living the way the military has taught you. Their way of thinking and that space you live in, when you come home from the military not knowing what your next step is in the civilian, real-world you will likely have some sort of PTSD. I had those moments several times as I transitioned home from the United States Air Force but also PTSD coming from jail. What was I going do with this felony? What was I going to do with this conviction? Some may say this will be so hard for a young adult to find a career. Well, I agree. What in demand job will hire a felon from the military? You do remember that I have to take care of myself and now my family? All I could think at the time was that my children are 3 and 4 years old, this is going to be tough. My family is growing and now I am thinking about getting married; a Wife and two kids to provide for. I was thinking that I was going to just work every job that hired me, no excuses. I was thinking of all of that deep inside, I had no idea what I wanted to do. I had no idea what I could do. I had no idea of what my limitations were. I did know that I was not going to stop until I was able to take care of my new family.

This step on who are you is important. It is the story that explains how you got where you are today. Everyone has a story, and everyone's story is important. The lessons that you learned, the obstacles that you went through, are what makes you who you are. This first step is the base of what the next nine steps will be.

NOTE:

STEP TWO

WHAT DO YOU WANT TO DO?

What do you want to do? No, really take a minute or two and answer that.

If you're not sure, it's ok. Remember, I was coming out of military with double PTSD, with a new wife, two children, and no career. Before I applied for a new job, or before I begin to update my resume, I really should be thinking of what do I want to do? But, 'what do you want to do?', is one of the hardest questions in the world to answer, when you really don't know. That question goes for your career goals and your life goals, what do you want to do? You really should write out those goals to check if they are S.M.A.R.T. goals. If you're not familiar, S.M.A.R.T. goals are goals that are Specific, Measurable, Achievable, Realistic, and Timely.

This is super important to do several times as you grow your career. The value that you get with this S.M.A.R.T. self-assessment will allow you to think through the career paths you will make and continue to grow. As you process your thoughts, let's think about the forever evolution of the mind. What happens is, the more you know, the more you grow. And the more you grow, the more you are subject to change your thoughts, which ultimately, changes your way of life. Most of us don't know what that change really looks like, so for me it was a process. I needed help finding me and I needed help finding my career. I always thought that maybe, if I kept working and being positive, that the career would find me. That led to me going through a phase of doubt, and self-sabotaging thoughts. where I would say the things that was holding me back was my PTSD, and how I could not get what one would like to call a traditional career track or career path, whether it be college, workforce training, certifications, or trade school.

The truth is most people in the world are in that same boat that I was in. Many people went through college and had some type of focused track with their degree. While others went through workforce training to have some type of dedicated track, it showed me that most people just go to work just go to work. Like myself, I ended up working in every career field that you can imagine.

I had no idea what I wanted to do. Over the years, I worked in just about every career field that there is. My friends and family thought I was crazy, they thought I was just job hopping, when the reality was, I really didn't know what I wanted to do. Let's run down my jobs; I worked in retail, I worked in grocery, healthcare, schools, transportation, hospitality, car salesman, I worked with utility company, grocery store, entrepreneurship, government, education, and landed in the nonprofit sector. It took all those things to find out what I wanted to do. But check it out, out of all that, I still ended up back to who I am at the core, something around the word "help".

I feel like if I went on a deeper thought, I would find a few more different jobs tracks in my arsenal. I had to really find myself and imagine what I could do for living if nobody paid me right now.

Next, I want you to think about it, what would someone say you would do as a career? What would be the right questions to ask you about your future career? How would you get into this field? How do you prepare to search for the job? What does your resume look like? These are some things that I learned through multiple job interviews. What have you done in your background growing up that can heavily influence what you can do in a profession? If you do not get the continued education, a trade or certification, it would be very hard to explore your options. Questions like, what did you like to do growing up, are limited to what you have seen. What was your personality like, can stretch further than your imagination ever could. What your personal life is like now is the difference. It offers you a chance to focus on what your strong points are, or what makes you smile every day.

What are you good at? What comes easy to you? I can only imagine if someone was asking the right questions early enough in my journey, whether that was in high school, transitioning throughout my career, or even later as a seasoned person in the workplace; I am certain that I would have added so much knowledge in my craft higher pay grade. When these types of thoughts and strategies are in place, you almost fall into your career. The chances of finding a career are heightened when you can be in field that you like and can do well.

Helping people find their career is what I'm great at, so make sure that you don't just follow the script with these questions, be sure to take a moment and create a system to track your effectiveness and your progress. Systems change your proficiency, proficiency changes your productivity, and productivity changes your pockets. I break the word system down to be this simple; S-save, Y-yourself, T-time, E-energy, and M-money.

Imagine you have to fill out an application form that has open fields that you enter pertinent information like your name, email, phone number, etc. If you were to leave one of them fields blank, do you realize how much time one would have to spend to find you to retrieve that information from you? The system was out in place for a reason, to capture that pertinent information upfront to help you move forward with the application process. Now suppose it was a scan database that the form would have to go to next. Your application, with the field missing, would not even make it pass the scanning process.

Remember that systems are in place to keep us accountable to things that we don't always have the answer to. In this case, they help people like me and you, find career options. If you take the time, whether you were a professional in the space of workforce development or if you were a person reading this for self-help learning yourself, check in and find out the key points that make you happy, and those things that you're good at. Once you find those things, you have to align them in the career path.

Let's take baking cakes as an example; if baking cakes make you happy and you're great at it, maybe you should start being interested in training as a Pastry Chef. As a Pastry Chef, here in the Washington, DC Metropolitan area, with no experience, the median income is $51,025 with the experienced median income of $89,632. Now I know you all make

$250K plus a year, so that's not much money for you and your family; this is entry level. And this does not include any gigs that you may have outside of your fulltime career, that can make you an enormous amount of passive income.

In comparison, still here in the DC Metropolitan area, your entry level teacher median income is $61,215 and entry level firefighter are at $54,550. Though these career fields are random, I wanted to share that searching for non-traditional careers is key for career exploration. You must find what you like and research that specific field. The money is there and will follow you as you master your craft. Be sure to use the steps you need for any training or certifications in your field to assure that you can be compensated for your professional expertise. Find out if certifications are required, or if specific work experience in that field is needed. You may have to work with a company as a W-2 employee or you can work in the growing Gig Economy as a 1099 contract employee. The Gig Economy is a free market system in which temporary positions are common and organizations hire independent workers for short-term commitments. Some gigger examples are driving for a ride share company, services under websites like Fiverr or TaskRabbit, Virtual Assistant, and tons of other gigs. To be a successful gigger you should train yourself to be adaptable and start thinking like a social expert.

There are some career fields that you can jump into. Whether you need credentials, or decided to be a full-time entrepreneur, you must research the route you are going to go and what steps are needed to become successful.

You are already past steps 0 to 1, you read up on Step 1 and you're now finishing Step 2. Just do yourself a favor, follow through with all action items needed to be successful. It will not be easy and do not underestimate the amount of work it will take for you to be successful in your space. You cannot skip any steps and expect to fully grasp the next step.

Before you go to the next step, sit down now, and figure out what your strengths are and what you're great at. You will be finding your path and you may have to come back to look at these. You will need help from a trusted person(s) to help you go through that process. You may or may not have the bandwidth to do it on your own but at least at some point reaching out to voice what you want to do, you can add some level of accountability to the conversation. Just know it won't be easy, though at times it may seem easy because you love it and it's fun, but you have to go through the process all the same.

So, let me ask you again, what do you want to do?

NOTE:

STEP THREE

WHAT ARE YOU GREAT AT?

In Step 3 you must think about what do you do at ease? Not like the last step of what do you want to do? Let's be clear, I want to be on the radio talking all day and make millions of dollars doing so. However, what I am great at or comes naturally is helping people; more detailed, is helping people find their careers. The question really is if you do it at ease, who says that you're great at it? You do know that you can't just say that you're great at something because you think you're great at, right? Who solidified you? Who vouched for you to say that you're great at something? Let's think about that once you realize how this thing comes easy to you. If you're a great writer and you feel like that it comes easy to you, who else confirmed that? Do people reach out to you on a regular basis and pay for you to write? Do you have regular written publications? Can your writing skills some way allow you to be considered for someone to ask for your help? How many people can you say that you have as a professional reference that you can use to say that you're the right person for the job?

Ok, so that comes easy to you, you have the reference to say that this is what you're great at; now how do you find a career with it? Just because you're good at it and it comes easy to you, just because you've been hired several times to do the job, does not guarantee that it's now your career. How do you turn that to a career, those are questions that you really have to ask, because once you're sure you like a field, and this is something that comes easy to you, people have solidified you in it, then turning that into a career is ideal, right? Remember don't cheat the system, trust the process. If you truly don't know that someone would say this is for you, then you may not be ready to turn this into a career. With that said, maybe it would be a hobby until you're fully ready to turn it over to a career. Being that this comes easy to you, you have to be careful on if you're on the search for the new career or if you are the one in position to be helping an individual mold into their own career. You could be the best point of contact for someone else and the career search is not even for you.

We've all heard the statement that goes something like, "once you find what makes you happy it won't be like going to work every day", well the truth is once you find something that comes easy to you, once you find something that you can do every day, and you were good enough to get paid enough money to take care of yourself and your family then it won't be like going to work every day. Let's be real, if you were only getting paid the very minimum amount, and the job made you happy, it would be rather tough to make it a career. On the other hand, if a job stressed you out and did not make you happy but you made $200 an hour, would you do it? Most would say yes, quick! The hard truth is that you would not make it to your full potential in life, you would never be happy, and would never find your N.E.M.O.

Great becomes natural to you when you think about what you're great at and what comes natural to you. I often reference a well-known gentleman that we call MJ. That man MJ can get confused or confusing depending on your state of mind. When I say MJ, your brain automatically goes to greatness because in today's world when we say MJ, we think either Michael Jordan or Michael Jackson. The funny thing is they both knew what they were great at, they both knew what came natural to them, and they both elevated. They took their careers to the next level once they found out what they were great at, and they practiced their craft every day. Michael Jordan played basketball every day, even as far back to when he got cut from the team in 9th grade basketball tryout.

He continued to practice because he knew he was great at it, and it came easy to him. He played other sports such as baseball, and was good at it, but what came easy to him was basketball. He focused so much on his craft that it got him to the next level of college, then the next level of NBA, and once he knew that was where he was, he didn't stop, he didn't just make it to the NBA; he is still in the space as an owner of a team.

The key is to do more, once you find out what you are looking for and what comes easy to you, even if you have not perfected or mastered it, do more. This is one of the things that everybody comes to you for input or advice on. Grow, Grow, GROW! Let your greatness live on far beyond your work. The same thing with Michael Jackson. For Michael Jackson this was singing, dancing, and entertaining. It came so easy to him that he was great at it far more than others. People told him and he began to excel. When he was with the Jackson 5, though he was younger than his brothers, he began to be the lead. He began to practice dance moves after others like James Brown and others began to sing more solo songs, he continued to grow and stretched his talents. Then every time you seen Michael Jackson; he was entertaining at the best that he could be.

How did they get to be so good? Did it really come easy to them or are they the best at it? Either way make sure that you practice your craft and get a good team around you. They both practiced and they both knew the value of a good team. I often think about the great Allen Iverson, aka "AI" or "The Answer", when he played for the Philadelphia 76ers. Allen Iverson was a flat-out athlete; basketball just came easy to him, and he was great at it. One of his most televised videos, off the court, is his comment about practice, "we talking about practice". He was the #1 draft pick, Rookie of the Year, All-Star MVP, arguably one of the greatest scorers in NBA history, and more. Now I know he practiced, and I know he knew he needed a team, but I truly believe that if he had spent more intentional time on the practice and the team efforts, that he would have gone even further in his legacy. Now I am not judging anyone's success, because to me he was one of many athletes that people looked up to. My entire basketball team had his shoes and dressed like him every day. We may not have had the success on the court without the likes of Allen Iverson. The older, professional me now can just see some of the opportunities that may have been left by not focusing more on the details.

So, as you are reading this, continue to grow, and focus on the details. Once you find that you're good at it and others say that you're good at it, then you're great at it. You have now found your job; you found the thing that you want to do. You are on your way to Finding Your N.EM.O. Now continue to go through these steps. As you know, the purpose of this book is for you to hear the stories, attach them to your life, and apply the steps. Ok, you know what you're great at and you know what comes naturally to you, you can now see a career; you have to figure out what's next! Let's get to it!

NOTE:

STEP FOUR
CAN YOU SUSTAIN THIS AS A CAREER?

Can you make money from any of your career choices? The easy answer is yes. We all know you can make money in almost any career field. Just about every career, provides some sort of a service. And that service that you provide, can make money. Selling dirt that's free from the earth, can make money to builders, in the lawn care industry, and so on. Doing back flips can make money, in entertainment, stunts, and so on. We are all in the service industry. You are either providing the service or doing something that adds value to the person who is providing the service. These are things that people want, and when doing things that people want, you can make money. Now that you understand that is just about anything, but can you make the money, the tough question? Can that thing be sustainable for what you would call a career? Can you make the money long enough to take care of your responsibility for yourself and your family? That's where we're going with this step. Though you know who you are, you're happy, and it comes easy to you; can you make enough money to survive?

You should do a real gut check to see if you can make money in this career. Sometimes it's like you want to do something, you're good at something, and you know what you know, so you know that it's safe to go to this job and then boom, they pay you agree to is just not enough money for you to survive. What do you do now? The amount of money you need just did not match the money you see on that paycheck.

Even if there is retirement there in the future, you will have to be working for 25-30 years, and not be happy. Being happy, those things that come to your mind are important and can affect your body. If nothing else, eventually you'll just be upset with anything career related. So, what you do is you start telling other people in your family and your friends the same thing. Sometimes you don't know it, or maybe you haven't been taught how to find it, you end up just falling back and not looking for the opportunities. With a little research, market analysis, reaching out, and some other things we are going to learn later on here, you can find a way to chase your passion and be able to take care of yourself along with your family forever.

It's something that you love, so don't take a lot of time to do the research; you should already have a peaked interest to know how to search for what you need. If you do not, you should reevaluate what you considered as your passion.

Check to see if there are other people in the space, do a Google search to see if there are careers in this space that you're good at and be greater. The more research you do, the more you'll find, and the more you'll feel comfortable in that "don't know" state. You will soon realize that sometimes what you know vs. what you don't know can stunt your growth until you are searching in the space of intentionality. This research process is a huge part of life where people are afraid to go. Most are afraid because they compare, they self-doubt, and they have imposter syndrome. A few methods to help with this are to take small steps at a time with your time, evaluate your abilities, and get out of your own way; separate yourself from everything and finish what you are starting right now. It's that place of separation from which one is in fear to fail, and we all know that fear is false evidence appearing real. That fear stops you from being great, it stops you from finding N.E.M.O., that passion, that thing that should be and could be your career. So, what I really want you to know is take fear out and think, can you do this job forever? I'm talking physically, mentally, and of course financially. If that answer is yes, you can, then do the research.

The research will let you know if you're able to make this passion, this thing that comes easy to you, a career. Once you are sure that you can then it's sustainable. Let me be clear, sustainability is all you need! If you can sustain a period of time, I mean years of time dedicated to this craft, then it's your career and there is more money to come.

To a hammer, everything is a nail. So, to you, you may feel like this career is the best career in the world. Remember, you have to know if you could sustain in this career both mentally and financially before you spend the time and energy exploring. There is no reason to get yourself excited to only put yourself in a state for the empathy fatigue that's in front of you.

If you know you can't do this forever, it's not your career for life. I would say think of the worst thing about that career opportunity. If you can see yourself in the worst day, and the worst moment of that career, and still have some sort of happiness to do the work, then that is it. If not, you have to rethink and reevaluate if this is for you, and that is ok. You would revisit this step and continue when it's your time. You would then have to do a market analysis of where you live or where you plan to work if you're working from home. Does the market show a trend that you can be doing this to make money for yourself and your family for years to come? If it does not, you may have to find a supplemental income, a part time job, or another career track to be sustainable. Now this does not mean that your plan and your new career will not work with your S.M.A.R.T. goals. And we know S.M.A.R.T. is Specific, Measurable, Attainable, Realistic, and Timely. You're S.M.A.R.T. with your goals but you have to know if you can actually maintain this new career as you transition into it.

NOTE:

STEP FIVE

WHO ELSE IS IN THIS SPACE?

This one sound easy, but is it? Well, go ahead and find them then. Find them and write their names down. Write down their story. How long did it take for them to get on the level that they are on? Write down everything that you know about them. After that take some time and cross-reference yourself. Check to see where you line up with them. Now we know people say, "don't compare", but for this one step, do just that, compare. If you don't stand up to them, it's ok; you are on the way of finding your

N.E.M.O.! If you do compare, sweet, this step should be a confirmation; take notes.

Research them with the determination of how to duplicate them. How do you say that somebody is successful in your eyes? How would you say that somebody is doing great, who has been doing this career for a long time? You would have to do some intense research on the person and the career. The reason for this research is that it allows your brain to think and allows your brain to search on other people outside of who you thought was the best in that career field. It's a chance for you to practice what I call, Mental Rehearsal. Mental rehearsal is when you mentally prepare for that one step back before it even happens. You prepare for it so you can stay focused on all of the positive things that you have going on, so that when things go wrong, you don't get bothered. You continue on with the process, focusing on what's in front of you.

Once you do this research, you will soon see that there are tons of people doing the type of career that you are now in the space of making your own. It will give you a chance to look at a couple websites, read about a few people through a google search, check their LinkedIn, and see what best practices have worked for them in the current state of that career. And once you find out the best group of people from your search, who are the top three people in the space? What makes them successful to you? Maybe it will be success in money, successful in visibility, or success in whatever viewpoints you see. You must learn how to duplicate those attributes and make them fill your shoes. This won't be a walk in the park; however, this may be the most pivotal step out of all 10. This is often the step that people would skip when they're searching for a career because it takes time, because it takes dedication, and because it's not always easy to do. And when you take a look at yourself, it's not saying that you're going to be that person you're duplicating, it's saying that you're going to take your characteristics and your strengths, then you're going to duplicate what they have done to merge with your strengths.

I've done this several times in the past and each time that I've done this I've learned something new. I have tried to make sure that I made myself as close as I can to be like the top three people in my career field. Thinking like these people is more than only thinking of how they ran their operations, but how did they build their team, and how do they make their money. If I can duplicate that, then I can multiply the process on how I can make it better. You may have to call a few companies and ask to speak to their marketing representatives, I mean, you may have to do tons of research, and you may have to do various analysis to compare what you're doing and what they're doing, to see if it can be something that you can duplicate over time.

This analysis can be simple or complex. You just need to be sure that you check their LinkedIn, company website, or any other social method that you can find them on. See what their credentials are, see how their education is layered, see what their work history looks like. Even then, I can guarantee you that you will have something that you will have to ask for help from somebody in this new space. Why not be someone that you have checked out on your own time.

To me, one of the definitions of a true boss is to recreate yourself, duplicate your process and teaching it to someone else. Right now, today, you are the someone else. Make sure that you are ready and available to be recreated. In order to become someone that you never been, you have to do something you never done.

The most important quality of a leader is responsibility. Break the word down response and ability. You have to respond; when you see something someone has done that you know works, have enough control to respond. Ask questions and assure that you are able to create the new you. Next, is ability; you have to have the ability to recreate it from your own viewpoint to deal with each situation presented to you. Put that all together, response and ability; you now have the definition of responsibility. Now, let me ask again, who else is in the space?

NOTE:

STEP SIX

HOW TO ENGAGE YOURSELF IN THE SPACE?

Ask for help! I mean, really ask for help! It's rather hard to do. You have to ask people who are in the space and people who are searching for their careers, both the same. The fact is, we don't know it all. The fact also is the more you know, the more you grow. So, let's jump in.

There is a reason why you are not where you want to be, yet; big on the yet. A lot of that may be just because you are not in the right space with the right people. If you want to be a lawyer, hang around the courthouse; if you want to be a teacher, hang around schools; you get the drift. You just have to show up and be present. Once you find the right space to be in, begin to utilize your first 5 steps as a toolkit with your elevator pitch.

An elevator pitch is a brief conversation to introduce yourself, provide a point, and make a connection. It's called an elevator pitch because it takes just about the same time that you would spend riding on an elevator with someone and you decided to make small talk to break the dead air of you both riding from the top floor to the lobby with a stranger. Avoid leaving the person in front of you stuck with "the what, that what" face by being intentional in your delivery and intentional with your ask. Remember to spark interest and be memorable all in about 30 to 45 seconds. Need an example here's mine – "Hey, I'm BJ Paige and I'm a Workforce Development Motivational Speaker. My favorite quote is Your Network Is Your Net Worth and I spend every day of my life helping people find their career for life. I would love to connect with you to see if I can add any value to you or someone else that you know. Here's my contact, where's yours?" That's my elevator pitch for you to check out, and I just dropped the mic.

Back to engaging yourself. As I was saying, use these 5 steps up to now - *Who Are You?*, *What Do You Want To Do?*, *What Are You Great At?*, *Can You Sustain This As A Career?*, and *Who Else Is In This Space?*. These are the tools you should use as you navigate and follow through with your new elevator pitch.

Find your Avatar and use them. Your goal is to be the best you that you can be. You may have to visualize yourself as them. Again, who's that person that you see as successful? Look at them as you see yourself doing what you know you can or should be doing. How can you make yourself do what they do to implement what you already know or what you're learning right now to be greater? With that Avatar, picture yourself talking to others. Picture yourself walking into a room for work. Picture yourself successful. How does your Avatar act? How does your Avatar complete task? The more you see yourself doing this, the easier this will be once you get all of your steps in order and move forward. By then, you would have already done this in your head, you would have already hit the winning jump shot with zero seconds left to win the championship in the finals. You would have already seen yourself win through watching your Avatar win.

There are tons of people in this career space of yours, there are tons of people doing the work, you and your Avatar have to separate yourselves from the average and be sure that you are the one to be chosen for your career. Soon, someone else would want you to be their Avatar so show up and show out.

NOTE:

STEP SEVEN

BUILD YOUR LANE

That story makes me think of my airplane analogy. I'm sure you all been on a plane or have seen or heard a story of someone on a plane ride. Before the plane takes off, the flight attendant says a few things. One of the things that my mind holds on to is what the flight attendant says on the plane, "in case of emergencies and the oxygen mask dropped, be sure to put your mask on first and secure it, before helping others...". If you missed the point, this is a reminder that you have to be sure that you are secure, be sure that you are prepared, and be sure that you are ready to help yourself before helping other people. In short, you may have to do it yourself and build your own lane.

Let's say you're in search of a job or career, the traditional route; there are a few things that you should be sure to do. To make your chances better to get the job, you have to be able to prove that you can do what you say you can do throughout the hiring process. Let's talk it out. You have searched for the job announcement and now you're ready to apply. You have to get your cover letter, your resume, be prepared for the interview, be chosen for the job, and then follow through with your job responsibilities. The objective of your cover letter is for the Hiring Manager to invite you to an interview. The purpose of the interview is for you to prove your worth to be more than just the words on your resume. Lastly, any follow-up conversations are to assure that your skills and personality are a great fit to the team and the organization.

Here's a tough conversation in today's world, especially with all of the pro self-worth, and know your value campaigns everywhere you turn; you may have to rethink what your social media presence, down to what your profile picture looks like. Your communications with everything you do matters when you're building your lane. One of the things you can think about and ponder on, is you are forever on an interview. That don't mean that you are actually sitting in front of somebody being interviewed and being asked questions about this career. But what I really mean is that somebody is always watching you. Somebody is always checking to see if you are living up to what your future resume that you will submit looks like. For instance, I knew that my end goal was going to be something in workforce development. Which meant that I knew that I had to get to the front of the room to be able to speak with groups to show them my expertise. I knew that I would have to get more growth, more certifications and more continued education in my area of workforce development. This would be workshops, different teachable scenarios, interviews, hiring processes, conferences, leadership roles for organizations such as Executive Directors, or anything that other people would validate that I am an expert in workforce development.

There is no way possible that I could have downplayed the endless amount of opportunity that was in front of me as I built my lane. You have to be able to say to yourself, hey, my end game is this job title; what do I need to build within myself to get there. Let's use Executive Director of a nonprofit, just for the conversation so this can make sense. You should be pulling every job description that you see that says Executive Director and combing that thing out. By combing it out you're going to find what is similar in these job descriptions that stand out which sound like you. Once you've combed all the things that sound like you out you are going to spend a dedicated amount of time a day, I normally say at minimum, an intentional 10 to 15 minutes a day, just to assure what is going to show on paper and that job description matches your resume.

Once you've got to the certain point where you've spent the time and feel that you are at a stop, and you've spent the time to be sure that your resume matches that job description on what you combed out as your strengths you're in good shape. "STOP" is an acronym that we used with my original nonprofit that I founded, Boys 2 Bowties, it stands for "Seek Time Or Pay". You have to seek time today to make your tomorrow just that much better. Right now, today, congratulations, you are seeking that time.

There are going to be things that you've combed out that are in your strengths or in your wheelhouse that may not be in that particular job description. Be sure to add them on your resume in a way that may view you as an overachiever in your space. I would be careful on putting those narrative bullets above those that are required for the career opportunity that you are applying for. Then, find your strength or in your wheelhouse that are separated from things that are still in the job description that don't really look like you. With those items that are in that job description that don't really look like you, you are going to have to prove to the hiring manager why you're the person for the job. You may have to take the direct certifications for the job description, take a smaller role in the company just to get that job descriptions verbiage to match your resume, but you are going to have to figure it out. Remember in Step 5, "Ask questions and assure that you are able to create the new you".

I was told once that no one is coming to save you. I couldn't agree more. So, if you want to save yourself and build your lane to make that job you, like that Executive Director career opportunity, there's going to be things you just have to do. One thing that you must work on are the small directions you make each day. Small directions can change the viewpoint of where you're going. I'd like to use the bowling analogy. You know everybody wants to be a bowler right, everybody is the best bowler they know. I don't care how good you are bowling, if you twist your wrist just a little or move your hand too far to the left, you're going to bowl the ball in the gutter. Those small directions change where the ball is going in the whole 60-foot lane. You will not get a strike with those 10 pins; you will miss the pins if you lean your foot to the right or the left a little too much.

You cannot change this destination tonight after reading this book; you'll have a lot of tools that can immediately help you for the future in finding your career for life. But you would not be able to change everything tonight. Here's what you can change today. You could change the direction of your thoughts. Even small directions of your viewpoints, the decisions in your discipline, the decisions from your learning, and decisions of your behaviors. These things will all change your habits which will ultimately change the directions of where you're going. Don't wish that things were easier, wish that you were better. Don't wish for less problems, wish for more skills. You have to add value to yourself to be sure that things are better as you build your lane. We all have gifts that's the superpower to the formula of your success. Focus on using them as a few disciplines and practice every day with what you have in you, for a better outcome. But those disciplines have to be well thought out, starting right now.

I just want to be clear, that building your lane would not be easy. It would not be something that you just wake up and do. It will be something that you will have to do repeatedly consistently and intentionally every day to show your worth and show how you can add value to every space that you get in. What's the one thing that you have in common with every person in this world? It's not the air you breath, look at mountain air vs. downtown city air. It's not water, look at some of the complications in Flint, Michigan vs. the popularity of water in Missouri. It's not even the blood in our bodies, the same blood types have different chromosomes which make our DNA different.

The one thing that you have in common with every person in this world is the 24 hours in a day. Even in different time zones, from Paris, France to Los Angeles, California; we all have the exact same 24 hours in the day. The quality of your life is determined by the quality of your time. If you want more, you do more. If you want a raise, you prove that you're worth the raise. You want that new position; you show your worth for that new position. The success starts with you, and you have to start it all by building your lane.

Now this is no secret to anybody reading this book, but you all know that you have to be consistent, and you have to add value as you build your lane. Remember to put your racehorse blinders on and do these three things to stay in your lane that you are building. Focus, factor, and finish. You have to show an intense focus with your blinders on like a horse in a race, so you only see what's in front of you as you build your lane. You have to factor how much time and energy is it going to take for you to be successful in building your lane. And then you have to finish what you start and Build Your Lane.

NOTE:

STEP EIGHT
KNOW WHAT YOU KNOW

Sometimes you just have to know what you know. It's funny when you really sit down and really listen to some of the workshops you attend, you realize that you knew this stuff. You knew it but didn't know that you knew it. Years ago, I attended a workshop where things were said that I didn't realize sat with me for so long. What was learned in that particular workshop is that life is simply circles. One circle is a huge circle as "you know what you know". For instance, I know that I am a great workforce development motivational speaker. Life is also a circle of "you know what you don't know". I know that I don't know how to change brakes on my vehicle, and for the record I'm OK with that, one of my jobs in my career for life journey was the manager of a well-known auto mechanic shops in the country; how ironic is that. Those are two circles of life. What's crazy is those circles are so super small compared to the huge circle of "you don't know what you don't know". There are so many things in this life that you just don't know that you don't know. And I know you're thinking like, "what is he saying?". What you are thinking also confirms why you don't know what you don't know.

That's the part that you have tapped into with Step 8; "know what you know"! You have to continue to educate yourself, build your career development and along with building your professional development. Stand strong in the circle of "you know what you know"; ask for help in the circle of "you know what you don't know; and forcefully chase the knowledge of "you don't know, what you don't know". Living in that circle is where you will learn the most, you will learn more than you could ever imagine. We all know the saying, the more you know, the more you grow. Do not be afraid of continued education through traditional education, training, workshops, seminars, certifications, books, and hey, even with "YouTube University". You will forever be learning, and forever be growing. Your name will continue to be in rooms that you never even entered.

Then the rooms that you will step in will be full of professionals where everybody is high-level, and you can stand in full confidence that you know what you know. That feeling of understanding what's being said and being able to speak on the conversation is a game-changer. As one of the experts in the space, you can now, again, add value to every situation that you are in. You want to be that person, the person that is getting an email or a phone call every day to be asked the question in the space, all because "you know, what you know".

NOTE:

STEP NINE

NETWORK

Network! So if this is your first time hearing from me this may be your first time knowing that my favorite quote in the world is "Your Network Is Your Net Worth". Your Network Is Your Net Worth is the last five people in your text message, your e-mail, your DM's, and your voicemail, they all show your value. Each time you pick up your phone and you see the last few people in your call log, they show your value and your worth; they show who you are and how you can get you to your new career for life. For those that do know me, you know you have heard me say your network is your net worth so many times that you may even not even know me by my name. Point to that is, the value of networking is as equal as the value of who you are. We've all heard the saying that everyone is 6 degrees of separation from each other.

In the professional world your craft cuts that in half to three degrees of separation. One who focuses on networking can cut that down to one or two people. I personally feel that if I really wanted to reach anyone that I see as successful, that I am one person away from reaching them. And I know somebody reading this book it's going to add even more value to my network, so I'll just say with ease that I'm 1 degree of separation from the likes of Oprah Winfrey, Jay-Z, Grant Cardone, Mark

Zuckerberg, Bill Gates, Jeff Bezos; from every person that I would call successful.

So, before we go any further in this step, I want whoever is reading this that can help me with that one degree of separation for me to get closer to any of the people, to just stop what you're doing right now and shoot me an e-mail to info@bjpaige.com to connect with me to any of those people to add value to my network.

That is a pure example of what networking really looks like in real time. You have to be intentional; you have to be direct, and you have to be humble enough to ask. The one piece that I didn't put in that is you have to show where you add that value. This entire 10 steps to finding your career for life is about adding value, building your career, and building you is like building your own network. It's like an entire separate brand that includes gaining your career for life, which will now follow you forever.

While building your own network think about it like life being a buffet. At a buffet you pay a price to enter, and you can sit down and wait for your server, or you can just get up and eat, which choice gets you to the food. If you wait for the food, nothing will be brought to you except for the bare minimum of utensils and drinks; but you paid to eat. You then have to get up and go get it.

Whenever you get up, there's a lot of options for you to get whatever you desire. You can get what you like, or you could try something new that you don't even know about, you can get whatever you want from the buffet. The kicker is you can get enough for just you to eat and you can bring back enough for everyone at the whole table. When you get back to the food you can get more of what you liked until you get full. You can always go back and get more, or you can always go and get something sweet for dessert. Networking is the same way; you can sit and wait for people, or you can always get up and go meet new people. You can then introduce the people you meet every day, to each other. The reality is, that if you don't get up from the table, you'll never be able to meet new people to try something new. Just go do it, meet new people every chance you get and be genuine with it. Remember this while on your journey; people care what you know, when people know that you care.

While you're at it, also remember not to tell yourself the stories. The stories that slow you down and hold you back. The stories that you tell yourself about not going the extra mile to network. The stories where you find that one successful person who says that they did it on their own, that did not have this and did not have that, and they still made it. The point is, if and only if that is true for them, they are not you. You need to build a team. As a matter of fact, a far majority of the people who made it to their level of success, did it through their network. You can now be a part of the snowball effect of success with your new network of people. Which brings the true definition to light of "Your Network Is Your New Worth".

NOTE:

STEP TEN
GO GET YOUR CAREER

Here's the million-dollar question, literally! How much are you worth? For one, you're worth this next career move! Remember, that the same .50 bottle of water is $2 at a convenient store, $6 at the airport, $10 at a nightclub, and $15 overseas on an exotic island. But the fact is, it's the same water, in the same bottle, with the same barcode. How? Why? The answer is that it's worth more based on the customer's wants and needs. You are that bottle of water. Know your customer. When you apply for this new career, speak to them as the person who has went through these 10 Steps, with confidence, and go get your career for life.

If nothing else have successful habits. The qualities or the characteristics of being a successful person are simple in my eyes. For one, have some clarity; the clarity of thinking clearly. It means the ability to determine exactly what it is you want to be. Be clear and decisive in your goals. If you don't know where you're going, any road can take you there. I hope you understood that. Keep fear away from you.

The acronym I use for F.E.A.R. is False Evidence Appearing Real. Fear prevents you from being decisive because you think you will make a mistake. However, the biggest mistake is creating the habit of not making a decision. You must have a dream, for a dream to come true. The best way to predict your future is to create it.

And have tough skin about it because truthfully nobody cares. As I said earlier, nobody's coming to save you. You have to develop to be conditioned for the race, for your race. In a race, there's a reason that the finish line is never close to the starting line. You have to be conditioned to run the race from where you are to finish the race. I mean just go get your career. These ten steps have now built you to do just that, finish the race.

If you can change your vision, you change your outcome. There are two things that you get every day a chance and a choice. If your eyes open, then God gave you a chance. You now have a chance to do something that you've never done before. Then the hard part is the choice. You have to make a choice to follow these 10 steps and to go gain your new career. Those are the choices that separate you from who you are today and who you will be tomorrow. Success starts with you!

Some people say you only live once, I disagree, you live twice and I'm living proof. Your 2nd life starts when you realize that you really only have one. In your career journey you will have to reintroduce yourself to yourself. It will be your own judgement that will cloud your vision, it will cloud your way to your goals. Just focus, if you focus on one thing, focus on one goal at a time, you will go get it! The universe will assure that if you focus on that one thing, you'll get it! Everything else you must let go. You have to have such an extreme focus on this career goal that it will be impossible not to succeed.

You are now equipped with the information and tools that you need to find your career for life. You can navigate and find the resources that ensure you know your strengths and how to make it as a career for life. You have the insight, you know how to research, you know how to insert yourself, you know where to look, and are ready to crush it!

The twisted truth is that you had this the whole time. You had the 10 steps in you, you may have even already started using them before reading this. But did you believe it? Did you know that you can do it? You have now found yourself! You are now empowered! You know your worth and you deserve your best career for life! Your Network Is Your Net Worth! You have now found your N.E.M.O. – New Employment Make Over!

NOTE:

NOTE:

THANK YOU

Thank you to my family for being with me through all of those hard times that I had as I was looking to find my career for life. They sat through 10 years of me finding myself and almost another decade of me perfecting my craft to where I am today. That's my Wife, my Children, my Mother, and my Friends; I cannot thank them enough. There has been a lot of blood, sweat, and tears to land where we are today. However, I am looking forward to building the next decade of success with them, for them. And thank you, yes you, for reading this right now, for trusting me as you continue your journey of finding, and sometimes sharpening, your career for life.

SHOUT OUTS

Super shout out to the US Air Force, Howard University, and Employ Prince George's. Out of the 20 plus organizations in my employment history, these are the three main entities that changed my outlook on what a career is today. It's just funny what the brain retains and how you apply it to your professional life. Even through it all, the US Air Force core values stand strong in my work ethics – *Integrity First*, *Service Before Self*, and *Excellence In All That We Do*. With Howard University, "*Truth In Service*", their core values are just as strong – Excellence, Leadership, Service, and Truth. I guess by now you can see the similarities. And Employ Prince George's for providing a person like me with no traditional degree, a felony from military law, and no previous experience on paper, to learn and grow into one of the top workforce development professionals in my lane throughout the country and heck, maybe even the world. I am thoroughly humbled and thankful to be where I am, and eager to be where I am going; can't wait for you to meet me there!

WHAT'S NEXT?
'HOW NOT TO GET FIRED?'

Everybody wants to tell you how to get a job, how about how to keep the career. Nobody really tells you how not to get fired. This next book will be a high level, "don't do" process of different scenarios with work solutions or how not to get fired. It will be another top seller. It will have intentional and clear examples of how to keep your job and further your career. It will leave you on the edge of your seat to go into your next duty day at work with a smile, high confidence, and the more tools for your toolbox that we all need to finalize our career. Three of the topics in this book will be, the Three C's:

1. Changing your perspective
2. Coordinating your position
3. Consecrate your passion.

You will learn how nobody fires people who execute, they fire people who work hard trying to execute. Stop trying and execute!

MY JOBS

- Mchunu House of Styles – Sales (Retail)
- K·B Toy Stores – Sales (Retail)
- Foot Locker – Sales (Retail)
- Long John Silver's – Food Services (Cook)
- Weis Markets – Stock Clerk (Grocery)
- United States Air Force – Security Forces (Military)
- Sheraton Hotel – Front Desk (Hospitality)
- Hollywood Casino – Security (Gaming)
- Sheraton Hotel – Night Audit (Hospitality)
- Last Stop – Sales (Retail)
- AIMCO – Leasing Consultant (Property Management)
- Washington Gas – Meter Reader (Utility)
- DARCARS – Sales (Automotive)

- Entrepreneur – Sales (Retail)
- Capital Entertainment Services – Fleet Manager (Transportation)
- St. Thomas More – Marketing Director (Nursing Home)
- Monsters Auto – Sales (Automotive)
- TitleMax – General Manager (Consumer Lending)
- Precision Tune – Service Manager (Automotive)
- Save A Lot – Store Manager (Grocery)
- Foundation School – Dedicated Aide (Education)
- Howard University – Executive Assistant (Education)
- Boys 2 Bowties – Founder, Executive Director (Nonprofit)
- PG EDC – Youth Career Consultant (Economic Development)

- Employ Prince George's – Youth Business Consultant (Workforce Development)
- Paige Group Inc. – Consultant (Workforce Development)
- Run Hope Work – Executive Director (Nonprofit)
- Baltimore-DC Building Trades Council – DC Metro Director (Labor Unions)
- Employ Prince George's – Returning Citizen Liaison (Workforce Developmen

MY BIO

Dr. BJ Paige is a Workforce Development Motivational Speaker who focuses on changing the lives of the youth. Born in Washington, DC and proud native of Prince George's County, Maryland; BJ is the county's first ever Returning Citizens Liaison under the Office of the Prince George's County Executive, Angela Alsobrooks.

He is a proven trailblazer in the field of Workforce Development, where he helps people find their career. He has numerous accolades to include specializing as a Motivational Speaker, Master Facilitator, Life Coach, National Association of Workforce Development Professionals (NAWDP) member and is a Veteran of the United States Air Force.

Newly named one of the DMV 48 Men of Power and the Greater Washington

Community Foundation Emerging Leader Award, the inaugural award of its kind, BJ serves the people in many roles. To name a few, BJ was a 2018 candidate for Prince George's County Council, District 7; he was named Top Forty Under 40 for Prince George's County; honored with The Maryland General Assembly Official Citation Awardee for his Community Commitment, presented the Real Good People Award WPGC 95.5, awarded the Citizen of the Year from Omega Psi Phi Fraternity – Gamma Pi Chapter, and a ton of honors to speak to his work in the community.

Additionally, with his focus on career development in higher education, BJ has worked as the Executive Assistant to the Health Sciences Executive Team at Howard University under the guidance of current President Wayne A. I. Frederick. BJ functioned as a Youth Career Consultant for

Prince George's Economic Development Corporation and Youth Business Consultant for the KEYS (Knowledge Equals Youth Success) Program at Employ Prince George's.

He has partnered with several civic based programs from feeding the underserved to re-entry programs for released offenders; Youth Advocate Programs (YAP); NAACP Youth Council Advisor – Prince George's County Branch, worked as the Executive Director for Run Hope Work, a nonprofit for at-risk young adults ages 20-24 in Washington, DC's toughest areas in Ward 7 and Ward 8, Founder of Boys 2 Bowties, mentor program with emphasize on helping young men grow from adolescence to adulthood; functioned as the DC Metro Director for the Baltimore-DC Metro Building Trades Council; and as the Associate Director, Flikshop School of Business, where they help prepare returning citizens for life as an entrepreneur in the gig economy.

"This book was brought about while on my journey to reach 100,000 Youth & Young Adults, #100KYouth. The goal was to give them some motivation and tools on how to finish school strong and focus on their careers now! Though we did not reach 100,000, we did reach 74,673! THAT WAS AMAZING TO DO! We felt that we could have reached more than the 100K, however we wanted to be intentional in our reach and offer more along the journey to assure that the youth had a sense of urgency on their options as they transition to their new careers as young adults. This book is what was comprised from that journey! So, thank you to all of the people who helped us reach so many future leaders of the world! We hope that you all now use this book as you are Finding Your N.E.M.O."

THE PAIGE GROUP

BJ PAIGE

www.ingramcontent.com/pod-product-compliance
Lightning Source LLC
Chambersburg PA
CBHW051105050425
24521CB00003B/3